CONTENTS

FLAT RACING

O LYMPIA IN ANCIENT GREECE is said to be the sanctuary of Zeus; today there remain statues, busts and ruins, as well as an incredible aura. The hippodrome, for horse and chariot racing, is long gone, but is believed to have been situated alongside the athletics stadium, which still stands. The hippodrome is thought to have been some 1,552 metres long (six 'stades') by 64 metres wide. The horses ran in races ranging in length between three to twelve circuits, and horse races and chariot races were included in the Olympic Games from 776 BC until the Games were abolished in about AD 393. The sense of wonder pervades: is this where it all started – this wonderful sport that we know as the Sport of Kings?

It was the Romans who brought horse racing to Britain, and to Yorkshire in particular, where the first recorded meeting was held at Netherby in about AD 210. Racing at that time was held in such high esteem that York citizens who wished to improve their social status used to give cash to meetings; the Greek Olympiads also relied to an extent on gifts of money, so sponsorship is far from new in the sport.

English kings have long played a part. King Athelstan (reigned 927–39) received a present of 'running horses' from France by a man called Hugh because he wanted to marry the king's sister, Ethelswitha. Henry II (reigned 1154–89) described races at 'Smoothfield' (Smithfield) in which 'jockies, inspired with thoughts of applause and

Opposite: Aerial photograph of the ancient racecourse of Roman Caesarea.

Greek vase
depicting a
chariot race,
c. 5th–6th
century BC.
Musée Municipal
Antoine Vivenel,
Compiègne,
France.

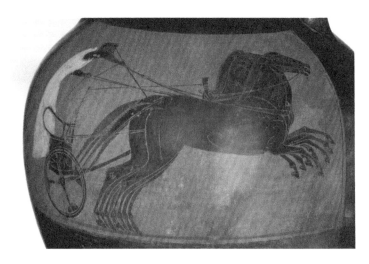

Flying Dutchman
winning from
Voltigeur at York,
13 May 1851. He
came from the
Darley Arabian
Sire line: King
Fergus Branch.
Flying Dutchman
was a talented
horse of the
highest class.
Run over two
miles, this match
was billed as the
'Match of the
Century'.

in the hope of victory, clap spurs to the willing horses,
brandish their whips and cheer them with their cries'.

Edward III (r. 1327–77) received two running horses
from the King of Navarre, and, just before Edward's death,
his grandson, soon to become Richard II, raced against the
Earl of Arundel. It was a match race (with two competitors
only) as racing was generally to remain for a few more
centuries yet.

The first fully established English racecourse was founded
on what is known as the Roodee, Chester, inside the city
walls in 1540 during Henry VIII's reign, and it remains

one of the most attractive of courses. York established its permanent course on the Knavesmire, outside the city walls, not far from the York Tyburn gallows. Courses began to spring up all over the country and races took place at many fairs and markets.

James I discovered that the heath around the new market near Exning was ideal for coursing and hawking. It was there on 8 March 1622 that, as an added diversion, Lord Salisbury and the Marquess of Buckingham matched their horses for £100, so founding Newmarket racecourse. During James's reign handicapping first came about – the system of allocating different weights to be carried by horses according to past performances. The system was designed to give all horses an equal chance of winning so that, in theory, they should finish in line abreast. Charles I continued the racing there but it was Charles II who really turned Newmarket into racing's headquarters.

In 1711 Queen Anne founded Ascot and put up a Queen's Plate, having come across a suitable place on the heath while following the royal buckhounds in her chaise. George IV was a great patron of the turf and won the Derby at Epsom in 1788, when he was Prince of Wales. Queen Victoria did not go racing but she kept the fine Royal Stud

The Round Course at Newmarket, Cambridgeshire, Preparing for the King's Plate, by Peter Tillemans, c. 1725.

Iroquois, ridden by Fred Archer, winning the Derby at Epsom Downs, 1 June 1881.

IROQUOIS WINNING THE DERBY.
Epsom Downs England June 1st 1881

Golden Miller, clearing one of the fences at the now defunct Derby, 21 January 1935.

at Hampton Court, and her son, later Edward VII, won eight Classics and a Grand National. George V won one Classic and his son, George VI, won four. Coming right up to the present day, Queen Elizabeth II has won four of the five Classics so far; only the Derby has eluded her, her Aureole finishing second in 1953 and Carlton House third in 2011.

The sport of kings it may be, but modern times have seen the birth of syndicates, where a number of people club together, spreading the cost and making owning racehorses financially possible – and occasionally profitable.

The early races were mostly matches or with three runners – usually owners wagering against each other, either riding themselves or paying someone more competent to do so, thus initiating the start of professional jockeys. By the time of Eclipse in the eighteenth century, races were mostly run in heats of up to four miles in distance, followed by a final, all on the same day. It is now established that horses may start racing on the flat from the age of two.

The first Classic to be founded was the St Leger in 1776, which introduced the concept of one race only, and which was over two miles long. Although a smattering of two-mile-plus races remain today the emphasis is

The 2,000 Guineas Stakes at Newmarket, 2 May 1934. Lord Glanely's unbeaten horse Colombo won from Eacton and the Aga Khan's Badruddin.

G. Bougourse
on Pourparler,
winning the
1,000 Guineas at
Newmarket, 30
April 1964.

increasingly on speed. The final race of the five Classics, the St Leger, no longer commands the prestige it once did, while one-mile-and-ten-furlong races vie with the more traditional mile-and-a-half races like the Derby for breeding purposes (buyers prefer speedier horses associated with shorter distances).

The Curragh
Racecourse, Co
Kildare, Ireland,
c. 1867.

The five Classic horse races in the UK are the Derby, the Oaks, the 2000 Guineas, the 1000 Guineas and the St Leger; they are the most prestigious and highest-class races. Ireland has its own versions of the same; all run at the Curragh, County Kildare. The Classics are all Group 1 races; the top races are graded Groups 1, 2 and 3, followed by Listed. The Irish Classics are run in the same sequence as those in the UK but on different dates so that it is possible for one horse

THE CURRAGH RACE COURSE
COUNTY KILDARE IRELAND

to run in both countries' events. The 2000 Guineas, the Derby and the St Leger are open to three-year-old colts, and all five Classics are open to fillies; it is the same in Ireland except for the Irish St Leger, which in 1983 opened its doors to male horses of any age, thereby letting in geldings.

The race for the Great St Leger Stakes, 1836, won by Elis, who was ridden by John Barham Day, trained by J. Doe and owned by Lord George Bentinck.

The most successful gelding has been Vinnie Roe who won the race four times from 2001 to 2004, and finished second in 2005.

The curtain-raiser to the Classics is the 2000 Guineas at Newmarket in May, followed the next day by the 1000 Guineas, for which only fillies are eligible. The Irish versions are run near the end of May. During the winter, or close season, there will usually have been a 'winter favourite' for both the Guineas and the Derby, based on their form in the two-year-old races. All four of the Guineas races in England and Ireland are run over one mile.

The Derby is the blue riband of flat racing, run over a unique and difficult course on the Epsom Downs in

The Lazarus stand at Doncaster on St Leger Day, 11 September 2010.

Surrey, south of London. For many years it was also the most valuable flat race in the world but these days there are others with bigger purses, such as the Dubai World Cup. Nevertheless, it is the Derby which retains the prestige as *the* race to win, and is usually run on the first Saturday in June. Along with the Oaks, for fillies only and generally run the day before, it is run over one and a half miles. The Irish Derby is usually run on the last Saturday in June, and the Irish Oaks is normally held late in July.

The world's oldest Classic is the St Leger, run at Doncaster, which was first held in 1776. It retains plenty of tradition; although it has been shortened, it is still the longest Classic horse race, of just over one mile and six furlongs. It is run in September, as is the Irish St Leger.

If a colt wins all three Classics for which it is eligible it is known as the Triple Crown. It is comparatively rare to win both the first two legs as a Guineas winner will often lack the stamina for the Derby, and a Derby winner may not have the speed for the Guineas, but in the 2010s there have been two notable exceptions in Sea The Stars (2010) and, two years later, Frankel. Before that, the last horse to win these two races was Nashwan in 1989. It follows that it is even rarer for all three races of the

Yves Saint-Martin on the French horse Monade, glances across at West Side Story, ridden by E. Smith, as they come up to the finish at the Oaks, 1962. The course judge awarded first place to Monade after consulting the photos.

Triple Crown to be won; in modern times it is seldom contested. This is to do with stud value and increasingly the St Leger is seen as appropriate for future National Hunt (NH) jumping stallions rather than for the mega-bucks world of flat-race breeding. The last Triple Crown winner was Nijinsky in 1970. In recent years only the Irish-trained Camelot has attempted it; he was odds-on in 2012 but finished second.

In theory, a filly can win all five Classics, whereas colts are barred from both the 1000 Guineas and the Oaks. The last filly to win the Derby was Fifinella in 1916, and the last to run was Cape Verdi in 1998. However, in 1902 Sceptre, one of the greatest fillies of all time, came close to winning all five Classic horse races, failing only in the Derby.

Leading up to or following on from the Classics are a number of top races: one is the ten-furlong Champion Stakes at the new Champions Day, Ascot, in October. It was moved from Newmarket in 2011; in that year its

Laytown Races on Laytown beach, Co Meath, Ireland. These authorised races are a unique event in the Irish and British racing calendar.

prize money was more than the Derby, but in 2012 the Derby was once again able to boast Britain's richest racing prize. Newmarket now holds a Future Champions Day in October, featuring the Dewhurst Stakes for possible future Classic contenders of either sex, and the Middle Park Stakes for future top sprinters or 2000 Guineas two-year-old colts only, run over six furlongs. The Dewhurst is the climax of the season for two-year-olds, run over seven furlongs of Newmarket's Rowley Mile. The Irish Champion Stakes over ten furlongs is held at Leopardstown in September.

The most prestigious race open to older flat racehorses is the King George VI and Queen Elizabeth Stakes at Ascot in July; it is often the first time three-year-olds will take on their older counterparts and can give an indication of ability between the ages, frequently with the current (three-year-old) Derby winner taking on the previous year's Derby winner; the younger horses receive a 10lb weight-for-age allowance. It is run over the Derby distance of one and a half miles. Fillies receive a 3lb allowance.

The Eclipse is a similar race open to all ages, run at Sandown Park over a distance of ten furlongs, a distance halfway between that of the Guineas and that of the Derby, and named after one of the sport's greatest stars and stallions.

Panorama of Ascot racecourse.

Horses with great stamina also have their chances on the flat with various top-class 'Cup' races, such as the two-and-a-half-mile Group 1 Gold Cup during Royal Ascot in June. There are a number of Group 1 Cup races at around two miles, while the longest race in the UK calendar is the Queen Alexandra Stakes, run over slightly more than two miles five furlongs as the final race of Royal Ascot in June.

Older horses of four years plus are also catered for at the highest level, including the Lockinge Stakes (one mile) at Newbury in May; the Coronation Cup (one and a half miles) at Epsom during the Derby meeting; and both the Queen Anne Stakes (one mile) and the Prince of Wales Stakes (ten furlongs) during Royal Ascot in June.

Two-year-old (juvenile) fillies have the Cheveley Park Stakes (six furlongs) and the Fillies' Mile, both at Newmarket in September. The one-mile Racing Post is the season's final top race for juveniles of either sex at Doncaster in October.

The season's concluding major handicap, the Cesarewitch, is run on the same day over a distance of two miles two furlongs; it is part of the 'autumn double' together with the Cambridgeshire, a one-mile-one-furlong handicap held at Newmarket in late September. The season's opening big handicap held every year in late March or early April is the Lincoln, run over one mile at Doncaster.

STEEPLECHASING AND HURDLING

Like the ancient Olympians, a diminishing band of genuine amateur riders still compete for glory. Global breeders like Coolmore and the Arabs race their progeny with a view to their becoming highly sought after stallions in the future, which will thereby generate massive wealth. But by far and away the biggest driving force behind racing is (as it has always been) betting. In fact, betting is how the comparatively new sport of steeplechasing began: in 1752 two gentlemen hunting in County Cork, Edmund Blake and Cornelius O'Callaghan, bet each other that theirs was the faster horse. They wagered a cask of wine on the outcome of racing from St John's Church, Buttevant, to St Mary's Church in Doneraile, a distance of about five miles.

The difference between this race and any that had gone before was that there were obstacles to be negotiated along the way: banks, ditches, streams, stone walls, and so on. History does not record who won, but Messrs Blake and O'Callaghan had begun something for posterity. Although originally a winter sport, steeplechasing now takes place all year round.

The sidekick to steeplechasing, point-to-pointing, has slightly smaller fences and is for amateur riders, and is usually run by local hunts or similar. Like steeplechasing – literally, chasing across country to a distant church steeple – point-to-pointing was originally run from one point to another, but today, like its big brother, it is run on a course that is

Opposite: Red Rum wins his third Grand National, 2 April 1977, the only horse in the history of the great race to win it three times.

Troytown, the winner of the 1920 Grand National, with jockey Jack Anthony at Aintree.

spectator-friendly and no longer has the cross-country element, with the exception of a few specialist races.

Hurdling is in between flat racing and steeplechasing, where horses negotiate hurdles which are smaller and flimsier than steeplechase fences; it is often the route taken by former flat racers, but it is equally the nursery ground for future steeplechasers. The hurdles were, until recently, always similar to sheep hurdles, but today a number of courses have a new design similar to a mini-chase fence, intended to be safer. But it was sheep hurdles which initiated the sport, and it seems that the Prince of Wales (the future George IV) may have been responsible. It is said he was out hunting on the South Downs, close to his ornate Brighton Pavilion and, sport being poor and spying some sheep hurdles nearby, some jumping matches over them ensued. The first official hurdle race took place shortly after, near Bristol in 1821. The sport was slower to develop and to be embraced by the authorities than steeplechasing but, as with that sport, it stemmed from hunting.

Horses can race over hurdles from the age of 'back-end' three, namely late in the year, not far short from being four-year-olds (all thoroughbred racehorses in the northern hemisphere have their official birthdays on 1 January). Some steeplechasers may race from the age of four, but, generally speaking, steeplechasers are slower to mature.

From its beginnings, as a result of a bet between two gentlemen in Ireland, steeplechasing has evolved into a high-class sport over set courses, the most famous of

Left:
Willie Robinson, remembered best for his association with Mill House, but who also won the 1964 Grand National on Team Spirit.

Right:
One of horse racing's legends, Sir Peter O'Sullevan, the commentator of the Grand National for over fifty years.

which – now also the most famous horse race in the world – is the Aintree Grand National. At just over four and a half miles and with thirty unique fences, it is a true test of greatness in a horse – and a jockey. Luck plays a part, and by coincidence its first winner, in 1839, was called Lottery. The Grand National at Aintree, Liverpool, is watched by 600,000 million – more than half a billion – people worldwide live on television. It is not the highest-class race because it is a handicap, but it produces the most interest. There is always a story connected with whoever wins the Grand National, one of the most outstanding being the previously crippled selling plater Red Rum, who remains the only horse to win it three times. (A selling race is one of the lowest grade; they do not exist in Ireland.)

The Grand National has come in for much criticism in recent times from people concerned about horses' welfare, but that is nothing new. It is worth noting that the vast majority of horses love what they do and relish the challenge of the mighty race; very occasionally a horse will not like it and will refuse to race; others rise above their normal racecourse form. In 1839, the very first year of the Grand National, there was a public outcry after a horse died, and mishaps at the five-foot-high wall resulted in this being

The Grand National Steeplechase, 1930. Glangesia is leading, with Toy Bell in the centre and Shaun Goilin, the winner ridden by Tommy Cullinan, at the top of Becher's Brook fence.

replaced for the third running of the race in 1841 by a water jump, which remains today, in front of the grandstands.

The Grand National meeting at Aintree takes place in early April, on a slightly flexible date depending on the date for Easter, and it has grown into a highly successful three-day festival. It has just one race each day over the Aintree fences, culminating with the Grand National on the Saturday; the Topham Trophy (over two miles six furlongs) is held on the Thursday, and Friday sees the 'amateurs' Grand National', the Aintree Foxhunter's Chase, over the same distance as the Topham.

Horses run towards Becher's Brook, Grand National, 2007.

All the other races are held over the Mildmay course and the principal chase is the Melling Chase on the Friday. The feature hurdle race is the Aintree Hurdle on Grand National day, the Saturday and third day of the festival.

As the conditions for the Grand National have been made somewhat easier, so some of the higher-class (and therefore higher-weighted) horses have contested it, but nevertheless the crème de la crème of steeplechasing for aficionados is the Cheltenham Gold Cup. This pinnacle of the jumping world is run 'on a level playing field'. Every horse in the three-mile-two-furlong event carries the same weight (the only exception being mares who have a 7lb allowance); that results in only the best horses contesting it, for a horse which in a handicap might carry only ten stone and still be beaten by the top weight there is no point in attempting to beat that same horse on level weights. The Cheltenham Gold Cup was introduced in 1924, eighty-five years after the Grand National, and for a number of years was a warm-up event for the Aintree marathon.

'The Madhatters' Race, Plumpton, Sussex, 1980. Prince Charles had his first race ride in this charity flat race, which was won by broadcaster Derek Thompson.

Monty's Pass with trainer's wife Mary Mangan after the Grand National, 2005.

Cheltenham, the 'headquarters' of NH racing, whose shop window is the four-day NH Festival each March, also hosts the top steeplechase for two-milers, the Queen Mother Champion Chase. This is for the speedier horses who may not stay the three-mile distance of the Gold Cup, and therefore generally makes for an exciting spectacle as the runners take the thick birch fences at a fearsomely fast pace. It was founded in 1959

Pat Taaffe on Arkle, taking the last fence ahead of Mill House at the Cheltenham Gold Cup, 1964.

and was given the Queen Mother tag in 1980 to mark the Queen Mother's eightieth birthday.

The hurdling crown belongs to the Champion Hurdle, run on the opening day of the Cheltenham Festival, and it has seen some outstanding winners in its time; some of them have come off the flat, and a few of them go on to be steeplechasers, but only one, the mare Dawn Run, has ever achieved the Champion Hurdle/Gold Cup double. The Champion Hurdle was founded three years after the Gold Cup, in 1927.

The King George VI chase is run at Kempton Park on Boxing Day and is run over three miles; the course is flat

The finishing line at Cheltenham racecourse.

and so this race does not require as much stamina as the Cheltenham Gold Cup nor quite as much speed as the 'Queen Mother' but is a top-class chase in its own right. Two horses have made it their own: Desert Orchid in the 1980s–1990s and Kauto Star in the 2000s–2010s. The race was founded in 1938 and for many racing fans it is their Christmas treat. This is a one-day meeting, whereas over in Ireland a four-day Christmas Festival is held at Leopardstown. The highlight is the Lexus Chase on day three.

Ireland also has its own five-day NH Festival, at Punchestown in late April/early May, about six weeks after its Cheltenham counterpart, and features Irish equivalents of the main Cheltenham races.

Punchestown was started by the Kildare Hunt in 1850, and in the next ten years became the headquarters of Irish steeplechasing. The first ditch or 'grip' of this famous double bank was 6 foot 6 inches wide and 3 foot deep; the top was 6 foot 6 inches wide; the second ditch, 4 foot wide; and the take-off was banked up. The whole 17-foot length was rarely, if ever, 'flown' in one leap.

Punchestown hosts Ireland's National Hunt Festival each spring.

BREEDING RACEHORSES

F ROM THE THREE founding fathers through Eclipse
and Northern Dancer and others to the scintillating
Frankel, breeding the thoroughbred racehorse is all about
speed and genes. Sometimes the best of racehorses fail to
reproduce their talent in their offspring, and occasionally
a cheap stallion will produce a star. Part of the fascination
of horse breeding is that it is not an exact science; if it were
the sport would be unlikely to exist because the winner
would be preordained and betting would be pointless, and
where is the excitement in that?

All thoroughbred racehorses stem from three founding
fathers imported from the Middle East during the late
seventeenth and early eighteenth century: the Byerley
Turk, the Darley Arabian and the Godolphin Arabian.
Fleet of foot, fiery and accustomed to desert terrain, they
also brought with them toughness, stamina and soundness.
They were crossed with the smaller and heavier type of
horse indigenous to England and Ireland that had been
used to carry men wearing heavy armour into war, and for
drawing carriages.

The first of the three founders was the nearly black
Byerley Turk, brought back after the 1686 Battle of Buda.
He went on to be Colonel Robert Byerley's charger in the
1690 Battle of the Boyne. He spent two years in Ireland
before returning to Byerley's home in County Durham,
and in later years north Yorkshire, where, from a limited
number of local mares, he produced offspring including

Opposite:
Sea The Stars,
ridden by Mick
Kinane, wins the
Derby, 2009.

Byerley Turk,
the eldest of
the three famous
founders of the
thoroughbred.

his most influential son, Jigg. Jigg sired Partner, and it was
Partner's son Tartar who sired Herod.

Foaled in 1758, Herod was leading sire eight times from
1777 to 1784; one of his most famous sons was Highflyer,
unbeaten in fourteen races and who usurped his father
as leading sire. In turn, his sons were champion stallions

The Darley
Arabian.

twenty-three times in twenty-five years, including Sir Peter Teazle, which brings us up to 1809.

The importance of the Byerley line was also established through other notable descendants, including the inaugural Epsom Derby winner, Diomed in 1780.

The second of the three founding stallions was the Darley Arabian, a fine chestnut who stood about 15 hands high. He is believed to have been smuggled from Aleppo, Syria, in 1704 by sailors on behalf of the British Consul Thomas Darley, after an agreed purchase at a price of 300 golden sovereigns fell through. The sheikh who was selling him reneged on the deal because, apparently, he could not bear to part with his finest colt.

Thomas Darley sent a message on to his brother, Richard, at the family's seat at Aldby Hall, near Leeds, hoping that the colt's exceptional quality would be appreciated by his fellow Yorkshiremen. It seems it was, for the Darley Arabian, believed to be from one of the purest of Arabian strains noted for their swift pace, became leading sire in 1722. He sired the undefeated Flying Childers and his unraced full brother Bartlett's Childers, who was the great-grandsire of Eclipse. Bartlett's Childers sired a number of top racehorses, including Squirt, who in turn sired Marske, sire of Eclipse. From a limited number of mares, mostly owned by the Darleys, the Darley Arabian was to become the most important sire in the history of the English thoroughbred: some 95 per cent of modern thoroughbred racehorses can be traced back to him via the Y chromosome.

The third foundation sire, the Godolphin Arabian (sometimes called Barb), was imported to England in 1728 (or 1729) from France by Edward Coke; there is a story (considered unlikely) that he had been pulling a water cart in Paris.

In his first year at Edward Coke's stud in Longford Hall, Derbyshire, he sired Lath, but only two years later Coke died, aged just thirty-two. He left his small group of mares

The Godolphin
Arabian.

and foals, including Roxana and Lath, to a personal friend
and fellow horseman, Francis, the 2nd Earl of Godolphin.
His stallions, including the Arabian, were left to another
friend, but in 1733, the Earl acquired the Arabian, which is
how he became known as the Godolphin Arabian. He was
moved to the Earl's stud near Babraham in the Gog Magog
Hills in Cambridgeshire, not far from Newmarket.

Lath was considered to be the best racehorse of his day,
and the best since Flying Childers, but the Godolphin
Arabian sired an even better one in a horse owned by
Lord Chedworth named Regulus (born 1739), who was
unbeaten as a racehorse and won seven King's Plates.

Regulus' most important daughter was Spiletta, dam
of Eclipse, while his most important son was Cade (born
1734), a full brother to Lath. Cade was inferior to Lath as
a racehorse, but vastly superior as a sire, and it is through
Cade that the male line continues down to the present time,
through Cade's son Matchem, who was a good racehorse
and excellent sire.

Racing itself has evolved through the centuries, but it is from the Byerley Turk, and the Darley and Godolphin Arabians that all today's thoroughbred racehorses stem.

One of the most influential lines in the last century was the Italian horse, Nearco (1935–57). He was bred by Frederico Tesio (who also bred the great Ribot) and was unbeaten, winning fourteen races at distances from five furlongs to one mile seven furlongs, proving himself to be more than a domestic horse by winning his last race outside Italy, in Longchamp, Paris. He proved himself even further as a stallion and sired Nasrullah, sire of the greatest horse to come out of Canada, Northern Dancer, who became one of the greatest of all stallions. He sired Nijinsky and Sadler's Wells, among nearly 150 Stakes winners and a dozen or so world-class stallions. These two were both trained in Ireland and stood there for their stud careers.

Although England has some high-class studs and breeders, notably around Newmarket, where both the National Stud and a number of Arab-owned enterprises are established as well as English ones, it is with Ireland that breeding is synonymous. The tradition of keeping one or two mares along with the cattle on the farm remains, and it is from similar origins that the mighty Coolmore breeding enterprise evolved. It was on a family farm that the Vigors set up a small training operation. After the Second World War ace fighter pilot Tim Vigors set about turning it into a model stud farm, laying the foundations for what is today a multinational business. Vigors brought in young trainer Vincent O'Brien, followed by Robert Sangster and Vincent O'Brien's son-in-law John Magnier; Tim Vigors sold his share and the rest, as they say, is history. Coolmore stands some twenty-three stallions at the stud near Fethard, Co Tipperary, and some of these shuttle to the southern-hemisphere Coolmore Farm at Hunter Valley, New South Wales, Australia, where about a dozen will stand during the season. About thirteen stallions stand at Coolmore's

Ashford Stud, Kentucky, USA. Stud fees for the Irish flat flag-bearers range from €4,000 to €40,000, with Galileo and Fastnet Rock listed as private (not available to the public). National Hunt breeders are accommodated via about fourteen stallions, whose fees in 2013 ranged from €2,000 to €10,000.

GREAT HORSES ON THE FLAT
SEA THE STARS

Sea The Stars was a model racehorse who was bred superbly, had excellent conformation, ground-devouring action and, most important of all, possessed a superb temperament. He set the seal on his career by winning the Prix de l'Arc de Triomphe at the end of his three-year-old season, a race that has proved a graveyard for many other great horses with otherwise unblemished records.

Sea The Stars was trained by John Oxx on the Curragh, Co Kildare, owned by Christopher Tsui and ridden by veteran champion jockey Mick Kinane. He was by Cape Cross out of Urban Sea, dam of Galileo; this mare thus bred two Epsom Derby winners; she also won the 'Arc' herself. Retiring to stud at HH the Aga Khan's Gilltown Stud, Sea The Stars produced his first two-year-old winner in 2013.

The only time Sea The Stars was beaten was on his racecourse debut, when he was a close fourth. Thereafter, Sea The Stars was invincible, despite the efforts of other top trainers. Unbeaten in six races at three years old, he became one of a select band to win both the 2,000 Guineas and the Epsom Derby, and he is so far the only horse to win the Arc in the same season as these two Classics.

FRANKEL

When Sea The Stars retired in 2009 he looked, in trainer John Oxx's words, perfect. 'He is the point to which thoroughbred breeding, after 300 years, has arrived.' Many in the racing world agreed that they were unlikely ever to

see such a horse again. And yet, only two years later, along came Frankel.

Unbeaten in fourteen races, Frankel was deemed a freak. He was also the ultimate tribute to the training genius of Sir Henry Cecil, because at first Frankel was too explosive for his own good. By the end of Frankel's career, which thankfully for all who love horse racing included remaining in training at four years of age, he was so laid-back that he actually lost about three lengths at the start of his last race; he was then given a race of it by the French-trained Cirrus des Aigles.

By Galileo out of Kind (by Danehill), he was never tested over the Derby and Arc distance of one and a half miles, and mostly ran over a mile, but from the way in which he surged ahead at the end of ten furlongs in his last two races the extra distance could have been well within his capabilities.

For many, Frankel's most extraordinary race was the 2011 2,000 Guineas at Newmarket. He went so far clear of the field early in the race that it appeared to spectators that he 'had to blow up and come back' to the rest – but not a bit of it; instead, he won by six lengths. This wasn't a case of the other jockeys being 'caught napping' – they were simply unable to catch up with him.

In every one of Frankel's fourteen races (ten of them Group 1) the superstar put up an exceptional performance; perhaps the most memorable of all was in the Queen Anne Stakes at Royal Ascot, which he won by eleven lengths at odds of 1/10 and after which he was rated the top Timeform flat mark of all time, 147. He was owned by Prince Khalid Abdullah, trained by Sir Henry Cecil and ridden by Tom Queally. He was retired to stud at Banstead Manor Stud, Suffolk, in 2006.

SEA BIRD II

Sea Bird II (known as Sea Bird), who won the Epsom Derby and the Prix de l'Arc de Triomphe in 1965, is headed only by Frankel in the Timeform ratings. His career was all the

Sea Bird II, with T. P. Glennon up, after winning the Grand Prix de St Cloud, July 1965. In the background are the horse's trainer, Etienne Pollet (wearing the trilby hat) and his owner, Jean Ternynck.

more remarkable because his sire, Dan Cupid, although second in the French Derby, was said by Julian Wilson to be 'inconsistent and volatile'; and he was out of a mare, Sicalade, who never won, and whose female forebears had never won. He was trained in France by Etienne Pollet and bred and owned by Jean Ternynk.

If Sea Bird's victory in the Derby was an effortless, scintillating display, his victory in the Arc was outstanding. In this he faced the French Derby winner Reliance II, the Irish Derby and King George winner Meadow Court, the American Derby and Preakness Stakes winner Tom Rolfe and, for good measure, the Russian Derby winner Anilin. In this truly international contest only Reliance appeared able to go with him, but then Sea Bird simply upped a gear and strode clear to a six-length victory.

In a career spanning eight races Sea Bird was only beaten once, and that was at two years by his better-fancied stable mate, Grey Dawn II, the leading two-year-old.

RIBOT

The 1950s saw one of the most remarkable of flat racehorses in Ribot. He remained unbeaten in all sixteen of his starts spanning three seasons. Bred, like Nearco, by the meticulous Frederico Tesio, he appeared unremarkable as a yearling and was not entered for the Italian Classics. Nevertheless, he ran up a sequence of victories in Italy which made him champion colt there at two, three and four years.

The real test of his ability came when he took on the best in France and England, twice winning the Arc as well as the King George VI and Queen Elizabeth Stakes at Ascot. After his first Arc, he beat an international field in the Gran Premio del Jockey Club, Milan, by fifteen lengths.

At four, he won over one mile seven furlongs in Italy, followed by the King George. His second Arc was even more impressive, leaving him to retire in style to stand at

Eclipse, unbeaten in eighteen races in the eighteenth century, painted when he was six years old by George Stubbs.

stud, firstly in England, then in Italy and finally in America.

His owner/breeder S. Tesio died just as the colt began his racing career, after which he ran in the name of the breeder's long-time business partner, the Marchese Incisa della Rochetta. He was trained by Ugo Penco and ridden by Enrico Camici. His Timeform rating is 142.

ECLIPSE

Going right back to the early days of horse racing, Eclipse was unbeaten in eighteen races; he was also a highly influential sire, and three of the first five Derby winners were by him. By Marske, he was a great-grandson of the Darley Arabian, out of a mare by Regulus who was by the Godolphin Arabian. He was bred by the Duke of Cumberland, and after the Duke died he was bought firstly by William Wildman and then, following a winning bet in which he placed 'Eclipse first and the rest nowhere', by Dennis O'Kelly.

Although half his races were walkovers, in which no rival was prepared to race him, in the 1760s a race would be run in heats of between two and four miles at half-hour intervals, followed by the final, so Eclipse covered many racing miles nevertheless. He also walked many miles between race meetings, as was the custom of the time. Eclipse was so far superior to his rivals that he was never fully extended.

A race named in honour of him, the Eclipse Stakes, over a little more than ten furlongs at Sandown Park, is the oldest Group 1 race, having been founded in 1886. Since 1976 it has been sponsored by Corals and continues to produce winners worthy of being mentioned in the same breath as Eclipse, such as Mill Reef, Brigadier Gerard, Sadler's Wells, Dancing Brave, Nashwan, Mtoto (twice a winner here), Giant's Causeway and Sea The Stars.

The skeleton of Eclipse is displayed in the National Horseracing Museum in Newmarket (on loan from the Royal Veterinary College). It was found that his heart weighed 14lb, about double the average at that time.

Arkle, taken by the author as a teenager with her Brownie camera.

NATIONAL HUNT HORSES
ARKLE

For most people, including the author, Arkle stands head and shoulders above the rest when it

Those with a special association with Arkle include Johnny Lumley (Arkle's 'lad', far left) and Paddy Woods (Arkle's work rider who also won on him, far right) and relatives of Arkle's trainer, breeder and principal rider. The author is pictured second left.

comes to steeplechasers. That is not to say there won't be some devotees of Golden Miller (five Cheltenham Gold Cups), Prince Regent and Arkle's own stable companion, Flyingbolt, but it is Arkle who remains at the top of the NH ratings. Not much was thought of him at first, but as he matured so he turned into a magical racehorse with a character to match.

He forced a change in the handicapping rules in both Ireland and the UK, whereby two handicaps were drawn up for a race in which a horse like Arkle was so far ahead of the rest; one list was for if he ran, with the other entries lumped near the bottom weight. Should the top weight not declare, however, the original list would result in an almost level, low-weighted race, so the second list came into effect, allotting weights across the spectrum for the remaining horses.

Arkle himself defied huge weights and all bar twice still won; his two other defeats came when he slipped badly in

his first Hennessy against Mill House, and when he broke his pedal bone in the King George VI chase at Kempton Park in what turned out to be his last race.

It is for his victories that Arkle is remembered. He bestrode the steeplechasing world like a colossus. Apart from his three Cheltenham Gold Cups he also won the Hennessy at Newbury twice, a King George and the Whitbread at Sandown, and he was unbeaten over fences in Ireland including the Leopardstown Chase (three times) and the Irish Grand National.

Arkle was bred by Mary Baker in Co Meath, trained nearby by Tom Dreaper for owner Anne, Duchess of Westminster, and ridden in all his steeplechases by Pat Taaffe.

FLYINGBOLT

Arkle's own stable companion, Flyingbolt, is rated only two points behind Arkle. He was more precocious, showing his amazing talent from an early age, and it was most regrettable that, in later years and for a different trainer, he kept running after a debilitating illness left him a shadow of his former self.

But from 1964 (when he won the Gloucester Hurdle at Cheltenham) to 1966 he illustrated his speed by winning the Two Mile Champion Chase (now the Queen Mother), and the very next day placing third in the Champion Hurdle – and yet he also had the stamina and weight-carrying ability to win an Irish Grand National the same year.

Flyingbolt was bred in England near Newmarket by Robert Way, owned by T. G. Wilkinson, and trained initially by Tom Dreaper in Ireland. He was pale chestnut in colour and, while he and Arkle were close in ability on the gallops, in the stable they were polar opposites: Arkle had the kindest temperament imaginable, but Flyingbolt by contrast was verging on vicious.

JOCKEYS

In the early years of horse racing owners raced against each other, but gradually the idea of paying a better rider (usually the owner's groom) to represent the owner on the horse evolved; these became professional jockeys. Often they went as apprentice boys to stables where they were indentured for five years. The apprentice system still exists, with special races for apprentices; when riding against 'fully fledged' jockeys they are entitled to a weight claim (the amount depending on how many winners they have ridden), but if an apprentice rides in a high-status race he will not be entitled to claim (and nor will an amateur). The apprentice equivalent in jumping is known as a conditional jockey.

Owners who rode themselves became known as amateurs, as were other riders who did not make their living from race-riding, instead, riding for the fun of it and not for money.

FLAT

FRED ARCHER

Fred Archer was quite possibly the best flat-race jockey of all time, but unfortunately he died at just twenty-nine years old. Fred Archer was born in 1857 near Cleeve Hill, overlooking Cheltenham Racecourse, and his father, William, was a National Hunt jockey (he won the Grand National on Little Charley the following year). At eleven years old, Fred Archer became a flat apprentice to Matt Dawson in Newmarket.

Opposite:
Ruby Walsh takes Irish Saint over hurdles in the first race at Festival Trials Day, Cheltenham, 2013.

Fred Archer on Ormonde.

Fred Archer, as depicted in *Vanity Fair*, 1881. The caption below reads 'The Favourite Jockey'.

Fred Archer was champion apprentice in 1872, and thereafter was champion flat jockey every year from 1873 until his death in 1886, riding a total of 2,746 winners, a record that stood until held by Sir Gordon Richards and then Tony McCoy. Tony McCoy was also champion conditional jockey the year before he began his long sequence of being champion NH jockey.

Among Fred Archer's twenty-one Classic winners were five in the Derby on Silvio, Bend Or, Iroquois, Melton and Ormonde. Probably his greatest feat of horsemanship was aboard Bend Or when riding with one arm (the other had been savaged), and just getting up to win.

Fred Archer was happily married to his boss's daughter, Helen Rose (Nellie), and he never got over her death in childbirth. This, coupled with severe wasting (he devised a purge known as Archer's mixture) and a fever, led him to take his own life.

GORDON RICHARDS

Flat-race jockey Sir Gordon Richards holds the British record for the number of races won in a career, at 4,870. Born in 1904, his record of 259 winners in one season (1932) stood for fifty years until beaten by jump jockey Tony McCoy. In 1933 he won twelve consecutive races.

Gordon Richards, still the only jockey to be knighted, was champion jockey twenty-six times; he won every Classic, eventually winning the Derby on Pinza in 1953, when he beat Elizabeth II's Aureole in her Coronation year.

Born in Shropshire, Gordon Richards was based for most of his career in Wiltshire, and is buried in Marlborough. Sir Gordon died in 1986.

LESTER PIGGOTT

Tall for a flat-race jockey, Lester Piggott devised a unique riding style with his backside poised high above the saddle; others may have imitated him but none could emulate him.

Born in 1935, Lester Piggott rode his first winner at twelve years old, and became a housewives' favourite and a nation's darling. He rode a total of 4,493 winners, spanning a career total of forty-eight years. He rode the winners of thirty Classic races, including nine Derbies, and was champion jockey eleven times. His Derby winners were Never Say Die (when he was only eighteen years old), Crepello, St Paddy, Sir Ivor, Nijinksy, Roberto, Empery, The Minstrel and Teenoso. He still rates Sir Ivor as the best horse he ever rode.

From a family steeped in racing, his grandfather, Ernie, won the Grand National three times, and his father, Keith, won the 1939 Champion Hurdle and trained the 1963 Grand National winner, Ayala. Piggott's cousins were flat-jockeys Bill and Fred Rickaby, and he married Susan Armstrong, a daughter and sister of trainers.

Lester Piggott riding Nijinksy to victory in the Dewhurst Stakes at Newmarket, 17 October 1969.

Frankie Dettori
performs his
famous flying
dismount off
Willing Foe after
winning the Ebor
Handicap at York,
25 August 2012.

FRANKIE DETTORI

Italian-born Frankie Dettori emerged on the UK and world flat-racing scene like a breath of fresh air. In 1990, when apprenticed to Luca Cumani in Newmarket, he became the first teenager since Lester Piggott to notch up one hundred winners in a season. Frankie Dettori's ebullience led to his renowned flying dismount off Group winners. The highlights of his career include winning all seven races at the Ascot September meeting in 1996. Frankie has won all the Classics, but it was not until his fifteenth attempt that he finally won the Derby, on board Authorized in 2007.

Frankie was born in 1970, and his father, Gianfranco, was Italian champion jockey thirteen times. Frankie has been UK champion three times, in 1994, 1995 and 2004, and has ridden more than 500 Group winners to date, including many abroad.

JUMP JOCKEYS
FRED WINTER

Fred Winter, born in 1926, was a horseman as well as jockey, and a man who always had time for other people. Effective and pugnacious in the saddle – he was champion

four times – he made the transition to training with immediate success, and was champion trainer eight times.

He is the only person to have both ridden and trained winners of the Cheltenham Gold Cup, the Champion Hurdle and the Grand National, but his best-remembered ride came in the Grand Steeple-Chase de Paris, (the French Grand National) at Auteuil, riding Mandarin. The bit in Mandarin's mouth broke, leaving him 'rudderless', Fred Winter had flu, and then Mandarin broke down (strained a tendon) – yet they still won the race.

He rode two Grand National winners, Sundew and Kilmore, and when he retired in 1964 he had ridden what was at that time a record of 923 NH winners.

Later the same year he saddled his first winner as a trainer – Jay Trump, who went on to win the 1965 Grand National. Fred Winter also trained Anglo to win the Aintree showpiece the following year. In all, he sent out 1,557 winners from his Lambourn stables in the twenty-four seasons until his retirement in 1988. His numerically best season was ninety-nine in 1975–76. Winter died in 2004.

Fred Winter on Halloween takes the last jump in the King George Steeplechase, Kempton Park, 1952.

Tony McCoy
after the second
race at Festival
Trials Day,
Cheltenham
Racecourse,
26 January 2013.

A. P. (TONY) MCCOY

Stan Mellor became the first jockey to ride 1,000 NH winners, but since then Tony McCoy has shattered all records. In 2013 he rode his 4,000th jumping winner. The previous record was Richard Dunwoody's 1,699. Tony McCoy has been champion jockey a staggering nineteen times consecutively. The previous record was seven. Richard Johnson has been runner-up to Tony McCoy on many occasions; he won the conditional jockeys title when he was eighteen in 1995, a year after his rival, and since that time has ridden more than 2,500 winners, yet never taken the title.

Stan Mellor, the first jockey to ride 1,000 NH winners, by the Dawn Run statue at Cheltenham.

A dedicated jockey in the mould of Fred Archer, Tony McCoy is always focused on winning, and also has to waste hard to make the weight. Born in Northern Ireland in 1974, he served his apprenticeship in southern Ireland with flat-race trainer Jim Bolger, and rode his first winner aged seventeen before moving to Toby Balding in the UK, who nurtured him at the start of his jumping career. He was conditional champion there in 1994 and has been overall champion ever since.

McCoy rode 289 winners in the 2001–2002 season, an all-time record under either code (flat and NH). Although he had won all the other main jumping prizes, the Grand National eluded him until 2010, when he won it at his fifteenth attempt on Don't Push It, trained by Jonjo O'Neill for owner J. P. McManus. The same year he became the first jockey ever to win the BBC Sports Personality of the Year contest.

BETTING

A PART FROM the thrill of breeding, owning, training and, in particular, riding winners, betting is the raison d'être for the vast majority of racegoers. We have seen that steeplechasing began as the result of a bet between two gentlemen out hunting; flat racing, on the other hand, most likely began as part of training for battle that probably evolved into competitions. It is probable that wagers took place almost from the beginning, and it is known that one William Hill operated a book on a three-horse race in Downpatrick, Ireland, in 1690. It is believed to have been won by the Byerley Turk, earliest of the three progenitors of the thoroughbred, a few weeks before he took part in the Battle of the Boyne. William Hill is believed to be an ancestor of the betting-shop chain founder.

In the seventeenth, eighteenth, nineteenth and even twentieth centuries betting gained a bad reputation because disreputable gamblers doped horses to lose races so that they could win on a longer priced horse, as well as engaging in other nefarious activities. Jockeys were not averse to rigging results for money, and in time were prohibited from betting. Racing's biggest 'clean-up' came with the establishment of the Jockey Club in 1750; the club drew up the Rules of Racing and administered these strictly.

Today, like the Rules of Racing, betting regulations have evolved and are also rigorously controlled, but greed is ever present, and racing authorities are vigilant

Opposite: Bookmakers at the Derby meeting, Epsom, Surrey, June 1960. Bookmakers are an integral part of British and Irish racing. In the majority of countries there is only a totalisator or equivalent.

Monday After the Great St Leger or Heroes of the Turf paying and receiving at Tattersalls, by R. Cruikshank, showing the quadrangle at Tattersalls filled with groups of betting men waiting to settle debts. Over the doorway is a sign which reads 'Horses must not be taken away without being paid for.'

in updating their efforts to keep the sport clean. Off-course gambling was not allowed until the first legal betting shops were opened in the UK on 1 May 1961; they opened at a rate of one hundred per week, and after six months there were 10,000.

It used to be the case that a bigger tax was deducted from off-course winning bets than on-course, to encourage people to go to the races. Betting is a multibillion-pound industry worldwide; in recent years online betting has taken a huge hold, severely reducing tax intake; nevertheless the

Epsom Races: The Betting Post, by James Pollard, c. 1934.

49

UK and Irish governments are in constant negotiations with the offshore companies to try to ensure that they contribute to the coffers.

The UK and Ireland, along with Australia, are, perhaps surprisingly, the only principal racing countries which have on-course bookmakers. Other countries operate only a totalisator or pari-mutuel system run by racing for racing; in other words, the profits go directly to help maintain racecourses (after government tax), whereas profits from bookmakers go to themselves. Bookmakers, however, are part of the colourful scene and tradition of Irish and UK racecourses, and are among the biggest and longest-serving sponsors of racing.

There are many different types of bets. In simple terms, the aim of the punter is to back a horse to win money, and the bookmaker offers odds according to the likelihood of a given horse doing so. If he considers a horse is likely to win he will offer short odds, and if he thinks it is unlikely to he will offer long odds. So at each end of this spectrum we can have an odds-on favourite and a rank outsider.

Starting with evens as a bookmaker's odds, this is where a winning punter who has staked £1 will win £1 (before tax); a 2-1 winning bet will earn the bettor £2 for each £1 staked, and so on, ascending. The Grand National at Aintree has produced five 100-1 winners in its 175-year history.

If a horse is considered more likely to win than evens his price will go into odds-on: that is, 2-1 on (or 1-2), in which case a punter will have to wager £2 in order to win just £1.

Basic bets are for a horse to win, or to place (to come in the first three, or two if there are seven or fewer runners). A place bet will usually be at a quarter or one-fifth of the

Betting on the Favorite, by W. L. Sheppard (from a sketch by W. B. Myers) and published in Harper's Weekly, October 1870.

win odds, because, of course, the chance of earning money is greater than win only; so a horse whose price (to win) is 8-1, may pay 2-1 if it places. Many bookmakers do not take place-only bets, but a tote or pari-mutuel will.

After win and place bets, the most usual is 'each way'. This is effectively two bets in one: a £2 stake is split into £1 to win and £1 to place (same horse). Another old bet is the forecast: to predict correctly the first two horses home (in order, or either order).

Over the years more and more varieties of bets have evolved. The jackpot is popular; this is run by the Tote (Totalisator, which operates in Britain and Ireland in tandem with bookmakers). In this a punter has to correctly forecast the winner of six races before the start of the first. This is an accumulator bet, in which the winnings from the first race are placed on the chosen horse in the second, and so on until, if the first five have won, all the accumulated winnings are then placed on the final selection. It's a bit like doing the lottery: it's extremely hard to win (some would say it's hard enough to find one winner, let alone six), but hope springs eternal when it comes to trying to win 'the big one' – and at least there is an element of skill in selecting winning horses compared with the random luck of the lottery.

Smaller accumulators are doubles, trebles and four-horse or more accumulators, which work the same way as the jackpot. Variations of these are bets like the Yankee, involving four horses but in multiple bets within the bet, namely, consisting of eleven separate bets: six doubles, four trebles and a fourfold accumulator. This is not dependent on all four horses winning or being placed, but a minimum of two selections must win to gain a return.

There are many other permutations of these basic bets in operation worldwide. Added to these, and with the advent of the internet and instant access to events generally, there is now also 'in-running' or 'live' betting. This allows the punter to place bets during the actual running of a race.

AT THE RACES

R ACE DAY for the punter probably begins with reading the racecard either in the newspaper or, increasingly likely today, on the internet. He will peruse the races – usually six or seven per meeting – study the form and make initial betting choices, before setting off for the race meeting.

Those involved with the runners – the trainer, jockey, lorry driver, head lad and lad – have considerably more to do; all that is required of the owner is to turn up. The owner doesn't have to provide the colours (silks) as these are in the care of the trainer and looked after by the valet. The trainer has to make a final declaration of his horse, and he is also responsible for saddling it.

The racecourse is run by a manager and the clerk of the course, who will keep the public informed of, for instance, the going. The handicapper will watch every race with a view to rating every horse's handicap mark. Keeping a careful eye on proceedings are the stewards, advised by a stipendary or professional steward, and they will enquire into any race where they feel there may have been a breach of the Rules of Racing. They are also aided by the camera patrol which came into use in America in the 1940s, and in 1960 in the UK.

After the race the placed jockeys have to weigh in, and once the clerk of the scales has checked that the winning rider has carried the correct weight an announcement will be made: 'weighed in' in Britain, or 'winner all right' in Ireland, after which winning bets may be paid out. The winning horse may be dope-tested afterwards.

Opposite:
Captain Lawson
escorting two
fashionable ladies
at Royal Ascot,
1934.

The final day
of Royal Ascot,
23 June 2012.

The jockey, who will have walked the course on his arrival, and may also have spent the morning in the sauna sweating off a last few pounds, is looked after in the weighing room by his valet. He is then weighed out by the clerk of the scales, to check that he is carrying the correct weight (including the saddle). The saddle is then handed over to the waiting trainer who takes it to the saddling boxes. Once the horse is saddled the lad then leads it into the main parade ring, and this is where racegoers get their first glimpse of the runners on the day. They can look at how well they look, how they walk and their apparent fitness before making their final betting choice.

The racecard helps many racegoers to choose which horse they want to wager on, but to the newcomer it can appear very confusing. If there is a figure in brackets beside a jockey's name, this indicates a weight allowance because the jockey is still a novice; initials in brackets after a horse's name indicate its country of birth if other than the host nation, for example, (USA); and the weight it is set to carry is indicated as, for instance, 11 10 (11 stone 10lbs).

Abbreviations such as 'bg' or 'ch m' stand for the horse's colour and sex, namely 'bay gelding' or 'chestnut mare'.

Crowds at Goodwood Racecourse.

A bay is a brown horse with black mane and tail as opposed to a brown horse (br) which is brown all over. A white horse is always termed a grey (gr); a chestnut is a rich, light brown, much like copper or the colour of auburn hair in a human. The racecard will also give the horse's breeding: by My Horse – Our Winner, gives firstly the name of the sire, followed by that of the dam. It will give the breeder's name as well as that of the owner, trainer and jockey, and will detail the colours to be worn. Many cards today also have this illustrated in a graphic, and may also give abbreviated form, that is, how the horse has run in its last three races, or an expert's opinion of its chances of success in the upcoming race.

Form figures 1, 2, 3, indicate placed first, second, third, in previous runs; F stands for fell, UR unseated rider, P pulled up, R for refused, RR for refused to race, and RO for ran out. BF indicates that on its last run the horse was beaten favourite; CD tells you that the horse has won over this course and distance before; all these are titbits to help the racegoer choose which horse to back.

Expressions can be confusing, too, such as hearing an owner say, 'My horse has got a leg.' The listener knows

A print (later hand-coloured) from *The Illustrated London News*, depicting luncheon time behind the grandstand, Royal Ascot, 1872.

horses have four legs, but not that 'having a leg' is horse-speak for a tendon injury; equally, he may be mystified to hear a horse is being 'ridden' as they all have jockeys, but

Queen Elizabeth II, with Prince Philip at her side in the royal procession up the course on the opening day of Royal Ascot, 1963. They were accompanied by the Duke of Beaufort and the Duke of Gloucester.

the term means the jockey is exerting all his strength to exhort the horse to go faster.

Because horseracing is perceived as the sport of kings it is often thought of as being elitist, for wealthy and posh people. That may have been the case in the days of King Charles II and to a degree until the Second World War, but this notion has proven erroneous over the years since then. The truth is that the whole spectrum of humanity can and does go racing including, thanks to syndicates and clubs, as owners.

It is the same with dress. With only a few exceptions a racegoer does not *have* to dress up to go racing; he may feel more at home if he does so but not necessarily. Some courses still have different enclosures, and smarter dress will be expected in the members' enclosure. With the advent of best-dressed-lady competitions at many meetings, some extraordinarily smart outfits can be seen out and about on otherwise ordinary days. Festival meetings that run over several days often have a Ladies' day, and this is another excuse to dress up.

Generally, racing is much less exclusive than it used to be, and many meetings have done away with different enclosures. Among various exceptions are Royal Ascot on the flat, and the NH Festival at Cheltenham. At Ascot there is still a strict dress code for the Royal Enclosure, but on the least expensive tickets, out on the heath, opposite the grandstand, you can wear whatever you like. Nevertheless, it is the tradition here for people to dress their best and enjoy the occasion – and their picnics – just as much as those on the other side of the track.

The first day of Royal Ascot 2012, with guests demonstrating twenty-first-century Ascot fashion.

RACECOURSES AND PLACES TO VISIT

THERE ARE sixty racecourses currently in Great Britain and twenty-six in Ireland, which includes two in Northern Ireland.

One of the great attractions of British and Irish racing is the diversity of the courses. Instead of only offering a flat, uniformed shape going one way round, these islands, the historic home of horse racing, offer a kaleidoscope of courses: some are small with sharp bends, others long and smooth; some have stiff gradients, others undulations, some are flat and even more are a mixture of these characteristics; some go left and some right; some are 'posh', while others are 'local'; almost all have history attached to them. Added together, there should be a course somewhere suitable for a given horse and its abilities.

Aerial view
of Chester
Racecourse.

Racegoers at the Craven Meeting, Newmarket, watch the horses in the parade ring.

The oldest racecourse is Chester, on the Roodee, dating from 1540, and in recent years the successful Ffos Las was opened in west Wales. In the UK many courses are for flat racing only, or for NH racing only, while a number are for both codes but on separate days, probably with flat meetings in the summer and jumping in the winter. Four courses have all-weather tracks alongside the grass: Lingfield Park, Kempton Park, Southwell and Wolverhampton.

In Ireland almost all the courses take both codes, and the codes are often mixed on the same day; the only exceptions are the Curragh, which caters only for flat racing, including all five Classics, and Kilbeggan in the Midlands, which has only NH racing. Dundalk has been Ireland's sole all-weather course since 2007 (it was a turf track from 1889 until closure for its redevelopment in the 2000s).

Newmarket in Suffolk is the 'headquarters' of English flat racing, and has two separate tracks. York and Ascot are both highly prestigious flat courses, and Ascot has also had jumping since the mid 1960s. Leopardstown, set in south Dublin close to the Wicklow Mountains, is the venue for Ireland's Champion Stakes on the flat and for a number of top NH races in the winter. Punchestown, in Co Kildare, hosts Ireland's NH Festival, while the Easter Festival at Fairyhouse features the Irish Grand National.

York Racecourse.

The northernmost UK course is Perth (NH); Hamilton (flat), Ayr and Musselburgh (mixed) and Kelso (NH) make up the Scottish courses. Ffos Las (mixed), Bangor-on-Dee and Chepstow are Wales' only courses. Northern Ireland is home to Down Royal and Downpatrick – these two courses illustrate the diversity in British and Irish racecourses generally: Down Royal is a long, almost square course suiting a galloping horse, whereas Downpatrick resembles a funfair switchback with some steep hills and tight turns.

England has courses in almost every part, with many south of London but almost none north/east of the capital – Great Leighs in Essex opened in 2008, but was forced to close; it remains possible that it might reopen. The furthest west is Newton Abbot (NH), and the furthest east is Yarmouth (flat), followed by Fakenham (NH).

Yorkshire is a popular northern racing destination, with ten tracks in this large county; it has well-known training grounds around Middleham. Lambourn on the Berkshire Downs is traditionally a NH training centre but with flat racing yards as well, along with the South Downs in Sussex, but the biggest training centre by far is Newmarket, mostly for flat racehorses.

In Ireland the Curragh is the principal training centre, but on an individual basis Ballydoyle, part of the Coolmore Stud operation in Co Tipperary, is world class.

Aintree Racecourse, Ormskirk Road, Aintree, Liverpool, L9 5AS.

Telephone: 0151 523 2600. Website: www.aintree.co.uk

Ascot Racecourse, Ascot, Berkshire, SL5 7JX.

Telephone: 0844 346 3000. Website: www.ascot.co.uk

Cheltenham Racecourse, Cheltenham, Gloucestershire, GL50 4SH.

Telephone: 01242 513014. Website: www.cheltenham.co.uk

Chepstow Racecourse, Chepstow, Monmouthshire, NP16 6BE.

Telephone: 01292 622260. Website: www.chepstow-racecourse.co.uk

Chester Racecourse, Chester CH1 2LY.

Telephone: 01244 304600. Website: www.chester-races.co.uk

The Curragh Racecourse, Co Kildare, Ireland.

Telephone: + 353 (0) 45 441 205. Website: www.curragh.ie

Doncaster Racecourse, The Grandstand, Leger Way, Doncaster, DN2 6BB.

Telephone: 01302 304200. Website: www.doncaster-racecourse.co.uk

Down Royal Racecourse, Maze, Lisburn, Co Down, Northern Ireland, BT27 5RW.

Telephone: 028 9262 1256. Website: www.downroyal.com

Downpatrick Racecourse, 24 Ballydugan Road, Downpatrick, Co Down, BT30 6TE, Northern

Ireland. Telephone: 028 4461 2054. Website: www.downpatrickracecourse.co.uk

Dundalk Stadium, Racecourse Road, Dundalk, Co Louth, Ireland.

Telephone: + 353 (0) 42 933 4438. Website: www.dundalkstadium.com

Epsom Downs Racecourse, Epsom Downs, Surrey, KT18 5LQ.

Telephone: 01372 726311. Website: www.epsomdowns.co.uk

Kilbeggan Racecourse, Kilbeggan, Co Westmeath, Ireland.

Telephone: 353 (0) 57 933 2176. Website: www.kilbegganraces.com

Leopardstown Racecourse, Leopardstown, Dublin 18, Ireland.

Telephone: 353 (0) 1 289 0500. Website: www.leopardstown.com

The National Horseracing Museum, 99 High Street, Newmarket, Suffolk, CB8 8JH.

Telephone: 01638 667333. Website: www.nhrm.co.uk

The National Stud, Newmarket, Suffolk, CB8 0XE.

Telephone: 01638 663464. Website: www.nationalstud.co.uk

Newmarket Racecourses, The Links, Newmarket, Suffolk, CB8 0TG.

Telephone: 01638 675 500. Website: www.newmarketracecourses.co.uk

Punchestown Racecourse, Punchestown, Naas, Co Kildare, Ireland.

Telephone: 353 (0) 45 897 704. Website: www.punchestown.com

York Racecourse, York, YO23 1EX.

Telephone: 01904 620911. Website: www.yorkracecourse.co.uk

GLOSSARY

amateur (rider): Unpaid jockey (officially).

back-end: End of the season.

breeder: The person who owns the dam of a horse.

by ... out of ... : 'by', the name of the sire; 'out of', the name of the dam.

code: National Hunt or flat.

colt: Uncastrated male up to three years old.

conformation: the way a horse is put together; how it looks.

dam: the mare; birth mother.

declare: The trainer declares a horse to run in a race.

evens: Equal odds

filly: Female horse up to three years old.

flat racing: Racing with no jumps.

furlong: 220 yards.

gelding: castrated male horse.

hand: 4 inches.

handicap: A race in which horses carry different weights according to their ability. A horse with good previous form will carry more than one with a less good record.

hurdling: Races in which hurdles are jumped (they are smaller than steeplechase fences).

leading sire: Sire who has bred most winners in a season.

length: A measurement in the result of a race, comprising approximately a horse's length.

mare: Female horse.

NH: National Hunt (jump) racing.

odds-on favourite: Considered so likely to win that one has to put on more money than one will win back (but if it wins one does get his stake back).

pedal bone: Bone in a horse's foot.

place (v.): To finish second, third or fourth.

plater: A horse that runs in the lowest type of race, a selling race.

point-to-pointing: Amateur steeplechasing.

racecard: Gives details of runners and riders for the day, along with other information including owner, and age, colour, breeding and past form of horse, etc.

rank outsider: A horse with long odds.

saddle (v.): To put the saddle on a horse.

sprinter: A horse that runs in a sprint race.

stade: Aproximately 258 metres (258.66 recurring).

stallion: An entire (uncastrated) mature horse.

steeplechasing: Racing over fences, usually made of birch.

stud: A stud usually houses a stallion and some mares.

stud fees: The mare owner pays a fee for the services of the stallion, for the mating.

stud (retiring to the): At the end of his racing career a colt may retire to become a stallion.

stud (stand at): A stallion stands at stud and mares are brought to him for mating.

yearling: A one-year-old horse.

FURTHER READING

Clee, Nicholas. *Eclipse*. Black Swan, 2011.

Herbert, Ivor, and O'Brien, Jaqueline. *Vincent O'Brien – The Official Biography by O'Brien*. Bantam, 2006.

Hillenbrand, Laura. *Sea-Biscuit: The True Story of 3 Men and 1 Racehorse*. Harper Collins, 2006.

Holland, Anne. *Arkle: The Legend of 'Himself'*. The O'Brien Press, 2013.

_____. *Classic Horse Races: Famous Moments from the History of the Flat, Steeplechase and Hurdles*. Marks and Spencer, 1989.

_____. *The Grand National: The Official Celebration of 150 Years*. Queen Anne Press, 1991.

_____. *Steeplechasing: A Celebration of 250 Years*. Little, Brown, 2001.

Maranti, Anna. *Olympia & Olympic Games, Myth & History, the Archaeological Site, the Museum, Modern Olympics, Posters and Emblems*. Editions M, Toubis, 1999.

Onslow, Richard. *Royal Ascot*. The Crowood Press, 1990.

O'Sullevan, Peter. *Calling the Horses*. Hutchinson, 1989.

INDEX

Published by Shire Publications, part of
Bloomsbury Publishing Plc.
PO Box 883, Oxford, OX1 9PL, UK
1385 Broadway, 5th Floor, New York, NY 10018,
USA

Email: shire@shirebooks.co.uk   www.shirebooks.co.uk

Transferred to digital print on demand 2017

First published 2014
First impression 2014

Printed and bound in Great Britain.

A CIP catalogue record for this book is available from
the British Library.

Shire Library no. 760.   ISBN-13: 978 0 74781 258 6
PDF e-book ISBN: 978 1 78442 004 8
Epub ISBN: 978 1 78442 003 1

Anne Holland has asserted her right under the
Copyright, Designs and Patents Act, 1988, to be
identified as the author of this book.

Designed by Ben Salvesen and typeset in Adobe
Garamond Pro and Gill Sans.

COVER IMAGE
Cover design & photography by Peter Ashley, racing
silks courtesy of Matt Mackley. Back cover detail from
a packet of Bar One cigarettes, collection PA.

TITLE PAGE IMAGE
Laytown Races on Laytown beach, Co Meath, Ireland.

CONTENTS PAGE IMAGE
Steeplechasing: *The Hurdle*, by William Shayer, 1869.

ACKNOWLEDGEMENTS
Author's collection, title page and pages 13, 19
(both), 23 (bottom), 21 (all), 23 (bottom), 35, 36;
Edward Betts/Wikicommons, pages 14–15; Library
of Congress, pages 8 (top), 10 (bottom), 40 (top),
45, 48 (top); Shutterstock, pages 11 (bottom), 22
(bottom), 38, 44, 54 (top), 55, 57, 60; Wikicommons,
contents page and pages 7, 48 (bottom), 50; Topham
Picturepoint, pages 6 (bottom), 9, 23 (top), 26 (both),
28, 34.

All other images are courtesy of Topfoto.

Shire Publications is supporting the Woodland Trust, the UK's leading woodland conservation charity, by funding the dedication of trees.

HORSE RACING
IN BRITAIN AND IRELAND
Anne Holland